THE WEB OF LIFE

Food Chains and Webs

Andrew Solway

Raintree

Chicago, Illinois

www.capstonepub.com
Visit our website to find out
more information about
Heinemann-Raintree books.

To order:
☏ Phone 888-454-2279
🖥 Visit www.capstonepub.com
to browse our catalog and order online.

Edited by Andrew Farrow and Diyan Leake
Designed by Victoria Allen
Picture research by Elizabeth Alexander
Illustrations by Oxford Designers & Illustrators
Originated by Capstone Global Library Ltd
Printed and bound in the United State by Corporate
Graphics

15 14 13 12 11
10 9 8 7 6 5 4 3 2 1

Library of Congress Cataloging-in-Publication Data
Cataloging-in-Publication data is on file at the Library of
Congress.

ISBN: 978-1-4109-4424-5 (HC) 978-1-4109-4431-3 (PB)

Acknowledgments
The author and publishers are grateful to the following
for permission to reproduce copyright material: Getty
Images pp. 32 (Flip Nicklin/Minden Pictures), 34 (Brian
J. Skerry/National Geographic), 39 (Tom Brakefield/
Digital Vision); Photolibrary pp. 5 (Malcolm Schuyl),
7 (Martin Harvey), 10 (Manfred Kage), 11 (Brigitte
Thomas), 12 (Kidd Geoff), 13 (Nick Garbutt), 14 (Doug
Perrine), 23 (Roberta Olenick), 37 (Richard Herrmann),
40 (Jacques Rosès), 41 (Mike Lane); Science Photo
Library p. 28 (Edward Kinsman); Shutterstock pp. 8
(© Pixeldom), 16 (© hunta), 17 (© Monkey Business
Images), 19 (© worldswildlifewonders), 21 (© 12qwerty),
24 (© Gregory Gerber), 27 (© Mogens Trolle), 29 (© Joy
Stein), 31 (© Matthijs Wetterauw).

Cover photograph of a male cheetah with impala
prey, Masai Mara, Kenya, East Africa, reproduced
with permission of Photolibrary (Fritz Polking/Peter
Arnold Images).

Every effort has been made to contact copyright holders
of material reproduced in this book. Any omissions will
be rectified in subsequent printings if notice is given to
the publisher.

Disclaimer
All the Internet addresses (URLs) given in this book were
valid at the time of going to press. However, due to the
dynamic nature of the Internet, some addresses may
have changed, or sites may have changed or ceased to
exist since publication. While the author and publisher
regret any inconvenience this may cause readers, no
responsibility for any such changes can be accepted
by either the author or the publisher.

Contents

Some words appear in the text in bold, **like this**. You can find out what they mean by looking in the glossary.

Making the Connections

Living things need food to stay alive. The way they get food creates connections with other living things.

Food connections

For example, let's say one animal (called animal A) eats another animal (called animal B). These animals become connected. But what if animal B had eaten a plant (called plant C) before it met animal A? When animal A eats animal B, it also eats the food (plant C) inside it. Or what if animal A also eats two other kinds of animals (animal D and animal E)? These living things are all linked.

Scientists talk about these connections by creating groups called **food chains** and **food webs**. In this book, you will learn more about how these groups and connections work.

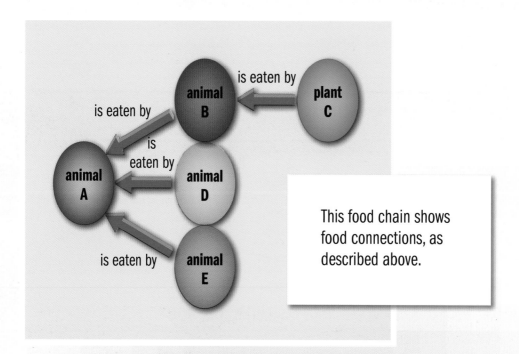

This food chain shows food connections, as described above.

WHAT IT MEANS FOR US

Wild bees help spread a plant substance called **pollen**. This helps plants to **reproduce** (make copies of themselves). In this way, bees help our food crops do well.

But in recent years, there have been fewer bees. Why? In Europe, farms have fewer wild flowers to feed the bees. In North America, a poisonous substance used to kill pests might be killing the bees. This loss of bees greatly affects other animals (like humans) in a food chain or web.

Plant-eaters and meat-eaters are all connected in nature.

WORD BANK
food chain group of living things that are connected through what they eat
food web group of living things that are connected through feeding

Energy

All living things need **energy** (the ability to do work). They use energy to move, grow, and stay alive. But where does this energy come from?

The Sun and plants

The Sun releases incredible amounts of energy. Plants are able to capture some of the Sun's light energy. They use it to perform a process called **photosynthesis** (see page 9). This process allows the plant to create its own food. The plant uses this food as an energy source to grow and live.

As we will see, plants are a major source of food for living things. When animals eat plants, the plants help provide the energy needed for life.

Everything on Earth gets energy from the Sun. Plants get energy directly from the Sun.

Ectotherms and endotherms

Living things need different amounts of energy to stay alive. Lizards, snakes, and frogs are **ectothermic**. They warm their bodies by soaking up heat from nature. Their body temperature can change over time.

Animals such as humans and birds are **endothermic**. They create heat inside their bodies. Their body temperature must be kept constant. This requires a lot of energy. Endothermic animals must eat a lot of food to get enough energy.

High-energy hummingbirds

Hummingbirds use more energy than any other type of animal. They eat their own body weight in food every day.

A lion chases a gazelle for food. The lion is endothermic. This means it needs constant energy from food.

WORD BANK
ectothermic describes an animal that needs to get heat from its surroundings to keep warm
endothermic describes an animal that produces heat within its body to

Producers

A **primary producer** is any living thing that can make its own food.

Plants grow in all kinds of surroundings. In dry areas, shrubs (small, woody plants) like these tend to grow.

Producers on land

On land, plants are the major producer. Plants make their own food through **photosynthesis** (see page 9). Plants are a food source. Food provides the **energy** living things need to survive. As a part of photosynthesis, plants give off something called **oxygen**, which is in the air. Many living things need oxygen to survive. So, plants are incredibly important for all living things.

Photosynthesis

Photosynthesis happens when a plant takes sunlight into its leaves. It uses the Sun's energy to combine water (sucked up through its roots) and **carbon dioxide**, which is in the air. This process makes **glucose** (a sugar). The plant uses sugars as food. Photosynthesis also makes **waste** (leftover) water and oxygen. These are sent out of the leaf.

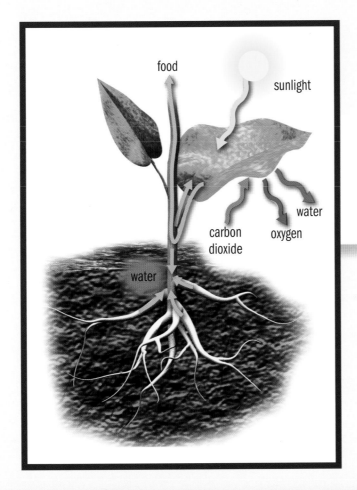

This diagram shows how photosynthesis happens inside a leaf.

Producers in the water

In the water, the biggest **primary producers** are plant-like creatures called **phytoplankton**. Most phytoplankton are very, very tiny. But they can grow in huge numbers. Like plants on land, phytoplankton are able to make food through **photosynthesis**. To get the light needed for photosynthesis, they must be near the surface (top) of water, where light gets through.

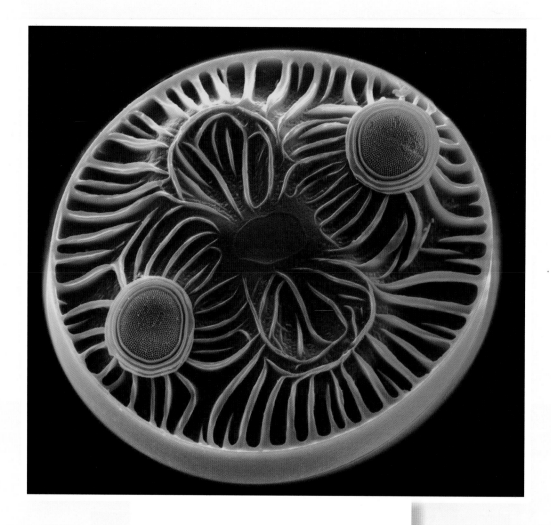

Tiny living things like this make up phytoplankton. This picture has been enlarged many times.

Unusual producers

In a few places on Earth, primary producers can make food without sunlight. Deep on the seabed, there is no light. But there are hot springs (areas of hot water) called **hydrothermal vents**. The water near these vents is rich in a substance called **hydrogen sulfide**. Some very tiny living things can use this special water to make **energy** and food.

Deep inside dark caves, a similar process happens. The air is full of hydrogen sulfide. This makes a rotten egg smell. Strange living things that look like long, white, gummy strings hang from the roof of the cave. They are called **snottites**. Using the hydrogen sulfide, the snottites make their own energy and food.

Killer plants

Some plants live in soil that has few **nutrients**. Nutrients are the parts of food that living things need to survive. Instead of getting nutrients from the soil, the plants get them by trapping and "eating" animals such as insects! This is true of the pitcher plant and the Venus' flytrap.

The Venus' flytrap catches a fly in its green, spiky "jaws."

WORD BANK
phytoplankton   very tiny living things found in the ocean, which are able to perform photosynthesis
nutrient   useful part of food that living things use to live and grow

Consumers

Consumers are living things that eat other living things to get food.

Primary consumers

Primary consumers are plant-eaters. Plant-eaters such as cows and zebras live by grazing (feeding) on grass and grassland plants. Other plant-eaters feed on different parts of plants, such as seeds, fruit, and wood.

Secondary consumers

Secondary consumers are animals that eat primary consumers. Many secondary consumers are predators (animals that hunt other animals for food). The most obvious predators are fierce killers such as lions and snakes. But many other animals are also predators, including ants and many frogs.

Many animals, such as bears, are omnivores. They eat both animals and plants. Omnivores are both primary consumers and secondary consumers.

Leaf miners are plant-eaters. They eat through leaves from the inside. This photo shows the tracks they leave behind.

The hunters

Predators hunt their **prey** (the animals they eat) in different ways. Some, such as cheetahs, chase their prey in fast sprints. Wolves are long-distance chasers. Eventually, the animal they are chasing becomes too tired to run further. Big cats such as leopards and tigers move slowly and silently. When they are close enough, they take their prey by surprise.

Predators like chameleons use **camouflage**. They use colorings and markings to blend in with their surroundings. This lets them surprise their prey.

Other consumers

A few animals are **tertiary consumers**. They eat animals that eat **secondary consumers** (animals that eat plant-eating animals). Some insect-eaters, for example, may eat insects that eat plant-eating insects. In the ocean, some large **predators**, called **quaternary consumers**, go one step further. For example, a shark may eat large fish. These large fish in turn feed on smaller fish. The smaller fish eat tiny sea animals called **zooplankton**. Finally, the zooplankton feed on **phytoplankton**.

Some sharks are
quaternary consumers.

Energy from food

Once food is in the body, we have to get **energy** from it. All living things, do this in the same way. They use a process called **respiration**.

Respiration happens inside a living thing's **cells**. Cells are the tiny building blocks that make up living things. In the cells, **oxygen** and substances from food (like sugar) are combined. This process creates energy. This energy powers everything the living thing does. **Carbon dioxide** and water are also released after respiration as **waste**.

Respiration is the "mirror image" of **photosynthesis** (see page 9). In photosynthesis, plants turn water and carbon dioxide into sugars. Respiration does the reverse. It turns sugars into carbon dioxide and water. Each process depends on the other for its fuel.

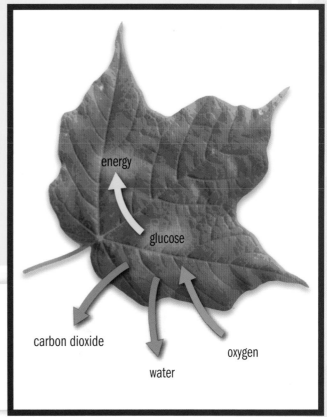

This diagram shows how respiration happens in a leaf.

Plant defenses

Plants cannot, of course, run away! But they do have defenses against animals that want to eat them. Many of them contain tough substances such as **cellulose** and **lignin**. Animals cannot **digest** (break down and use) these substances. So, they will not want to eat them. Other plants can make poisons to protect themselves.

The long thorns on this acacia tree are a defense against animals.

Some animals deal with these plant defenses. For example, cows and sheep have an extra stomach called the **rumen**. It contains billions of **bacteria** (very simple living things) that can break down cellulose.

WHAT IT MEANS FOR US

Humans eat many, many kinds of foods. Around the world, humans eat insects, snails, frogs, snakes, birds, and almost any kind of **mammal**. (Mammals are warm-blooded animals with a backbone. They have hair or fur. Pigs and cows are mammals.) We also eat many different kinds of plants, seeds, nuts, and fruit.

WORD BANK

cellulose   substance that is important in plant cell walls

lignin   tough, strong material produced in plants that is one of the main

A Simple Food Chain

A **food chain** is a way to write out and connect the **producers** and **consumers** in an area.

Connections in a chain

For example, in grassy areas called meadows, the **primary producers** are grasses. Mice eat grasses and grass seeds. The mice are food for snakes (see the art below). Changes in any step in the chain will affect the others. For example, the grasses could dry up from lack of rain. There would then be far less food for mice. Many would die. Fewer mice means less food for snakes. So, many snakes may also die.

Common confusions

Who's eating whom?

In diagrams that show food chains, the arrow always points toward the **living thing** that is doing the eating. One way to remember this is to think of the arrows as shorthand for "is eaten by...."

This is a simple food chain.

grass and seeds   mouse   snake   hawk

What if another animal comes into the food chain, such as a hawk that feeds on snakes? The number of snakes may begin to fall. Fewer snakes means fewer mice get eaten. More mice eat more grass and seeds. This could hurt the grassland.

These examples show how changes in one part of a food chain affect more than just one living thing.

This food chain shows the relationships between living things in a river.

Top of the heap

An animal at the top of a food chain is known as a top **predator**. Top predators might be a tiger, a crocodile, or a harpy eagle (like the one below).

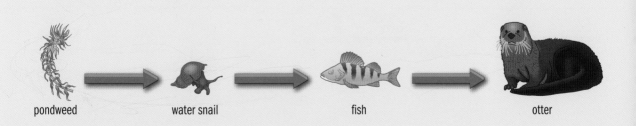

pondweed   water snail   fish   otter

From Chains to Webs

In nature, there is no such thing as a simple **food chain**. There are many other connections that make things more complicated.

Changing diets

Most animals change their diet if one kind of food is hard to find. For example, suppose a snake cannot find many mice. It might make up for this by eating frogs. This means that the animal is part of several different food chains, not just one. Together, these many chains form a **food web** (see below).

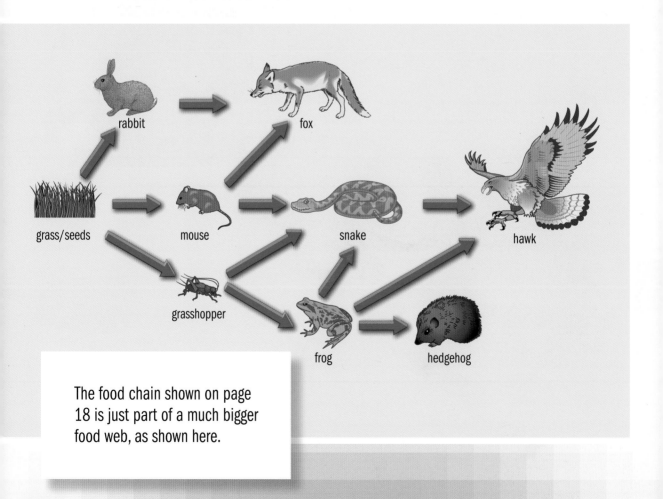

The food chain shown on page 18 is just part of a much bigger food web, as shown here.

Competition

If a food is good to eat and available, several different **species** (types of living things) may eat it. For example, the grasses in a grassland area feed many animals, from cattle to insects. Grass is widely available.

But some kinds of food are not always widely available. So, several species will compete for it. Often one species will win out. The other species may fall in numbers. Or they might switch to other types of food. They might also move to an area where there is less competition.

Red foxes will compete with other animals in the food web on page 20, such as snakes.

WORD BANK

species group of similar living things that are able to have young with each other

Finding a niche

Species can avoid direct competition. They can live in different places or eat different foods. One example is the feeding habits of birds that live along seashores. Different species of shore bird eat in different places and in different ways (see art below).

Sparrowhawks avoid feeding competition by growing to different sizes. The male is smaller than the female. It hunts smaller **prey**.

In this way, each species in a **habitat** (specific area) develops a particular way of life and of feeding. This is known as its **ecological niche**. If a species cannot find its own ecological niche, it will likely die out.

Different shore bird species feed at different levels of water. They also feed in different ways (look at their beaks). This avoids direct competition.

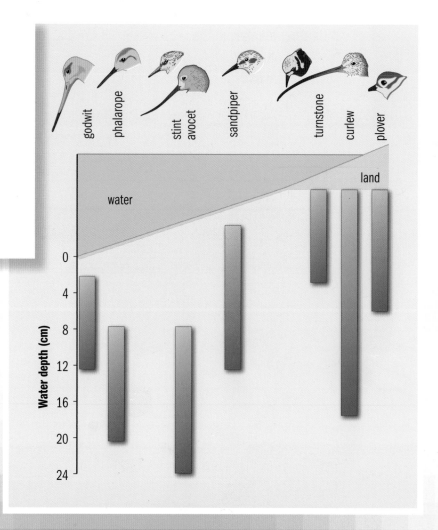

Food on the move

Many bird species spend the winter in warm areas. They then **migrate** (travel) to cooler places in the summer. The summer visiting place has lots of food for feeding their young. This solves the problem of limited food in the winter location.

Sea otters help to maintain their habitat.

Sea otters and kelp

Giant seaweeds called kelp form underwater "forests." These kelp forests are a good habitat for many living things. Sea urchins are animals that feed on kelp. Sea otters, in turn, feed on sea urchins.

In many areas, the number of sea otters has been reduced by hunting. Where there are few sea otters, the numbers of sea urchins increase. When this happens, the kelp forest can be eaten away. Clearly, changes to one species affect a whole **food web**.

Food Pyramids

When we eat an apple, our bodies use **energy** from it. But we only use some of the apple's energy. We do not eat all of the parts of the apple, such as the core. Our body also gets rid of much of it as body **waste** (see page 28).

A biomass pyramid

A **biomass pyramid** shows the waste that happens in a **food chain** or **food web**. This waste can be viewed in terms of lost **biomass**. Biomass is the total weight of living material in an area. (The weight of trees in a forest is an example of biomass.) A lot of biomass is wasted in a food chain or web. It is never used to create energy.

When we eat meat, we don't usually eat the head, skin, or hooves. We don't get every bit of energy that it offers.

Look at the biomass pyramid below. The bottom section shows the biomass of all the **primary producers** (plants) in an area. The section above this shows the biomass of all the **primary consumers** (plant-eaters). This is much less than the biomass of the plants. Why?

First, the primary consumers only eat one-fifth of all the plants available. Second, animals lose a lot of their food (95 percent) as waste. In the next step, the **secondary consumers** (**predators**) experience similar losses.

So, the animals at the top get only a tiny fraction of the biomass available from the plants at the bottom. The food chain changed from 40,000 tons of biomass (at the bottom) to 12 tons of biomass (at the top). This lost material cannot be used to create energy.

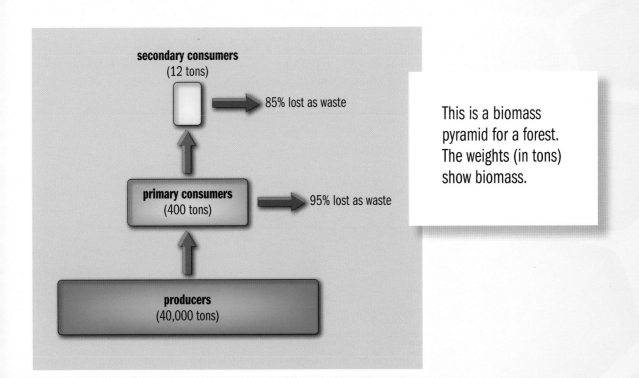

secondary consumers
(12 tons)

85% lost as waste

primary consumers
(400 tons)

95% lost as waste

producers
(40,000 tons)

This is a biomass pyramid for a forest. The weights (in tons) show biomass.

Biomass, energy, and number pyramids

The three "pyramids" below all look at the same woodland **habitat**. The pyramid on the left shows **biomass**, as we saw on page 25. The pyramid in the middle looks at **energy**. It is similar to the **biomass pyramid**. This is because less and less biomass (living material) is available to make energy at each step.

The "pyramid" on the right shows how many living things there are for each step in the chain—for example, how many birds. The section for **primary producers** is much smaller than the section for **primary consumers** here. But why? The primary producers are trees. One tree can feed thousands of plant-eating insects.

These are pyramids of biomass, energy, and numbers of living things for a woodland habitat.

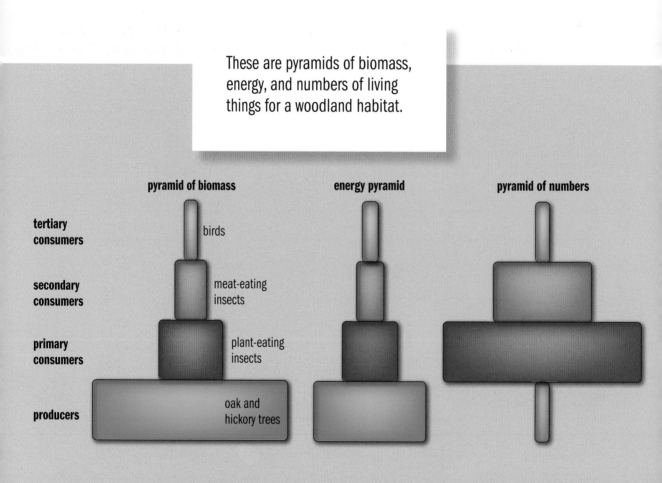

pyramid of biomass · energy pyramid · pyramid of numbers

tertiary consumers — birds

secondary consumers — meat-eating insects

primary consumers — plant-eating insects

producers — oak and hickory trees

WHAT IT MEANS FOR US

To raise an average-sized cow, it takes about 8 to 15 tons of plant food. After the animal is killed, we only eat about half its weight. The rest goes unused. So, should farms simply grow plant crops for food, rather than for raising animals? Would this create less **waste**?

It is not quite that simple. When we grow a field of wheat, for example, we do not eat the whole crop. We use the seeds (usually to make flour) and throw the rest away. Also, plant food is not as easy to **digest** as animal food. So, we have to eat a lot of plants to get enough **nutrients** from them. What do you think? Should we all be **vegetarians** (plant-eaters)? Or does meat have its place?

Lions need a lot of food. It gives them energy for running like this.

WORD BANK

digest break food down into simpler substances that can be taken into the body

Using Up the Waste

As we have seen, a lot of **energy** from food is lost between the steps of a **food chain** or **food web**. What happens to the energy? Living things use some energy to move around. They also use it to perform life processes, or actions, such as making body heat. But a lot of the food animals eat ends up as **waste**. It ends up as **urine** (liquid waste) and **dung** (solid waste). It also ends up in the air as **carbon dioxide** (see page 15).

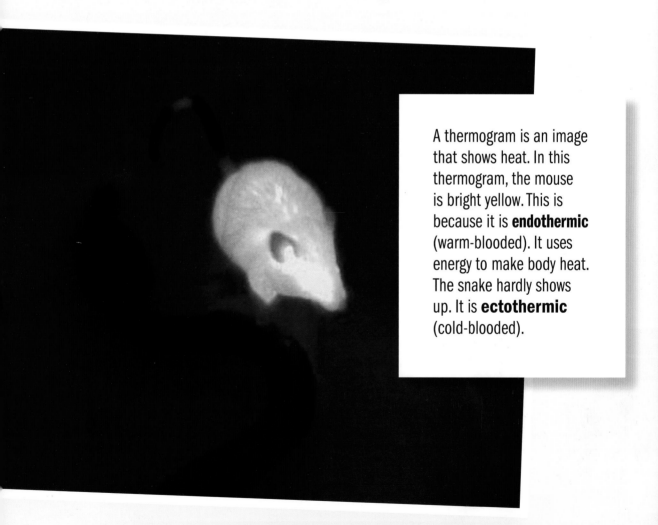

A thermogram is an image that shows heat. In this thermogram, the mouse is bright yellow. This is because it is **endothermic** (warm-blooded). It uses energy to make body heat. The snake hardly shows up. It is **ectothermic** (cold-blooded).

Living on waste

Animals called **detritus** feeders survive on the waste products of other animals or plants. Detritus includes urine, dung, dead plants and animals, and plant parts. Larger detritus feeders include beetles, flies, snails, and earthworms. Termites eat the leaf litter on the floor of a forest.

Detritus

In some streams, leaves and other plant parts drop into the stream from nearby plants. They collect in the riberbed. As this detritus breaks down, it turns into a kind of food. This food is eaten by small **primary consumers** such as water snails. These then become food for fish and other **secondary consumers**.

Dung beetles are the clean-up group of the animal world. They feed mainly on animal dung.

Decomposers

"Rotters," called **decomposers**, also break down **waste**. But they create useful materials from the waste. **Bacteria** are decomposers. So are **fungi**, especially for rotting wood. (Fungi include mushrooms and molds.)

Full circle

Bacteria and fungi break animal and plant waste down into very simple substances. On land, these substances may be released into the air or become part of the soil. They act as **nutrients** that can be taken up by plants. In the oceans, these simple substances help **phytoplankton** to grow.

In this way, the nutrients come full circle. First, they were used by **producers** to make food. Then, they became waste. Finally, decomposers broke them down. They made them enter the **food chain** again.

This diagram shows how decomposers fit into a food chain. The Sun creates **energy**. Producers use the energy to make plants. **Consumers** feed on each other and use this energy. Producers and consumers then create waste. Decomposers break down this waste. They get nutrients from it. They then return the nutrients to the soil, air, or water.

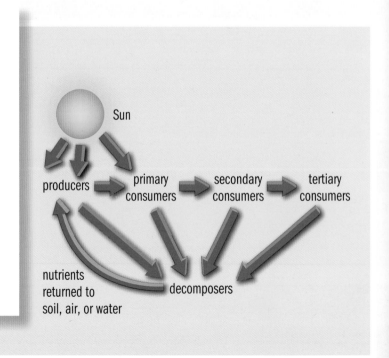

These fungi have formed on a dead tree.

Insect clocks

Scientists have done many studies on how dead human bodies rot (break down or fall apart). When a dead body is left out in the open, insects and other creatures are quickly attracted to it. Over time, different insects come to feed at different stages. Scientists examine which insects are living on a dead body. This tells them roughly how long the body has been dead.

WORD BANK
decomposer living thing that breaks down waste material and gets nutrients from it
fungus (more than one: **fungi**) type of living thing that includes mushrooms

Antarctic Food Web

Antarctica is a huge, empty wilderness covered in ice. There is little life in the middle of this land. But living things near the sea do survive. Overall, there are far fewer **species** in the Antarctic than in other parts of the world. This makes it an easy place for scientists to study the **food web** that exists there.

Important shrimps

At the center of the Antarctic food web are small, shrimp-like animals called **krill**. Krill live in the sea. The krill are **primary consumers**. In the summer, they feed on **phytoplankton**, which grow in huge numbers.

In winter, ice forms on the ocean surface. Conditions above the ice are incredibly cold. But under the ice, conditions in the water are not too harsh. Many living things can survive there in winter. As light begins to return in the spring, tiny plant-like living things called **algae** begin to grow. They grow on the underside of the ice. The krill feed on them. The krill eat and grow. By the time the ice melts, there are huge numbers of them.

This shows krill scraping algae from sea ice.

This is a simple version of the Antarctic food web. The different-colored arrows show different levels of **producers** and **consumers**.

- The phytoplankton are the **primary producers**.
- They are eaten by the primary consumers, the krill.
- The krill are eaten by **secondary consumers**, such as penguins.
- The **secondary consumers** are eaten by **tertiary consumers**, such as leopard seals.
- The tertiary consumers are eaten by **quaternary consumers**, such as whales.

A food web is not as "neat" as a **food chain**. Different animals end up connecting in different ways. Sometimes steps are skipped. For example, krill are eaten directly by blue whales.

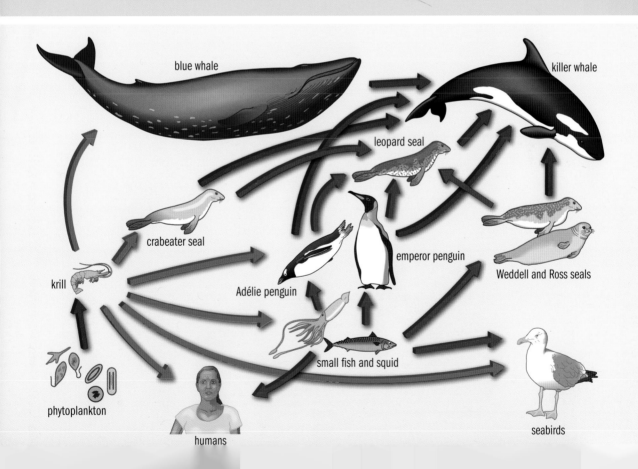

Feeding frenzy

The huge numbers of **krill** provide food for many other animals during the Antarctic summer. Some **species** eat almost nothing else. Examples of these species include some fish species, penguins, and some whales. These krill-eating fish provide food for larger fish, penguins, and whales. Humans also catch many varieties of fish. (See the **food web** on page 33.)

Instead of teeth, whales like this one have large, stiff plates. The plates filter small animals like krill out of the water. They let the water itself pass through.

plate

In the Southern Ocean, killer whales hunt penguins and sometimes even young whales. Leopard seals are also fierce hunters. They prowl mainly in shallow waters, looking for penguins and smaller seals. Southern elephant seals are also **predators**. They are deep-sea divers.

Keystone species

As we have seen, krill are central to the Antarctic food web. Any changes in the number of krill can have large effects on other species in the web. The krill are what is known as a **keystone species** in the Antarctic. Keystone species are animals or plants that are very important in a particular **habitat**.

Scientist have identified keystone species in other habitats. For example, in some tropical forests in South America, fig trees act as keystone species. These trees produce fruit all year round. A species of starfish is a keystone species along rocky shores of northwest North America. This starfish feeds mainly on mussels (a kind of small seafood). When the starfish is removed from the habitat, the mussels take over. They cover the shores completely. They force out most other species.

Constantly Changing

Habitats change all the time. Whenever these changes happen, **food chains** and **food webs** are changed, too.

Natural changes

The weather is the cause of many natural changes in habitats. For example, changes in rainfall can lead to crops not growing well. Fruit-eating birds may not be able to feed their young. The result could be that there are fewer birds.

Changes caused by humans

Human action affects habitats through fishing and hunting. If humans catch too many of a certain kind of fish or animal, this affects the local food chain or web. For example, the **predators** that eat that kind of fish or animal might go hungry.

Shrinking habitats

When humans build towns and cities, or clear land for farming, this also damages or destroys habitats. As a natural habitat shrinks, there may no longer be enough food in the area to support top predators. They also cannot find partners, so they do not **reproduce**. Eventually they may die out.

WHAT IT MEANS FOR US

We transport food around the world. This creates a human-made food web. Changes to one of the connections in this web has wide-ranging effects. For example, in the summer of 2010 lack of rainfall damaged the wheat harvest in Russia. Then, in late 2010 and early 2011, the wheat harvest in Australia was damaged by floods. As a result, the cost of bread, breakfast cereal, and other foods went up. This was because wheat was harder to get.

Bluefin tuna are a very popular food in Japan. Because of too much fishing, the **species** is close to dying out.

Global changes

Pollutants are substances in our surroundings that can cause illness and death. Some pollutants remain in the body. These kinds of pollutants can build up in a **food chain** or **food web**. If one living thing eats another thing with the pollutant, it takes in the pollutant. This process continues up the food chain (see below).

DDT

In the past, a substance called DDT was sprayed on crops to stop pests from eating them. DDT can be deadly for animals. When **primary consumers** ate plants sprayed with DDT, the substance built up in their bodies. **Predators** that ate primary consumers with DDT developed even larger amounts of it. At each step in the food chain, the amount of DDT built up.

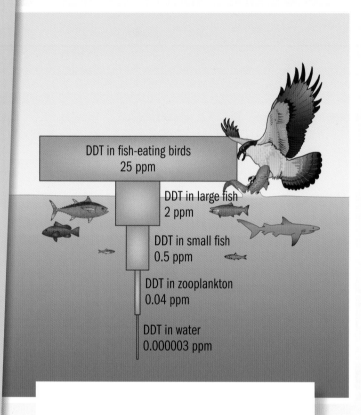

DDT in fish-eating birds
25 ppm

DDT in large fish
2 ppm

DDT in small fish
0.5 ppm

DDT in zooplankton
0.04 ppm

DDT in water
0.000003 ppm

This shows how pollutants increase as you go up a food chain. The abbreviation *ppm* stands for "parts per million." So, the larger the number, the greater the amount of DDT there is.

Ups and downs

Changes in food supplies can make the numbers of some animals go up and down over time. An example is the snowshoe hare. These plant-eaters live in northern North America. In years when there is plenty of plant food, hare numbers grow rapidly. But eventually there are so many hares that the **habitat** cannot support them. They do not have enough food sources. As a result, the number of hares falls greatly. The same pattern affects their predator, the lynx. The number of lynxes goes down if there are not many hares to eat. The numbers go up when there are plenty of hares.

Snowshoe hares are the main **prey** for lynxes.

WORD BANK

pollutant substance in an area that can cause illness or death in living things

Conclusion

We often hear on the news that a **species** of insect or a plant is in danger of dying out. But why does this matter?

There are over 35,000 different species of this kind of moth. If one species died out, would it really matter?

Biodiversity

As we have seen, humans actions are changing **habitats**. Over time, these changes reduce **biodiversity** (the number of species in an area). In a habitat with few species, changes in one link can have a large effect. **Predators** may not have the option to move on to different species of **prey**. As one species dies off, so will the next species that feeds on it. These losses might never be repaired.

WHAT IT MEANS FOR US

In the 1990s, the numbers of white-backed vultures in southern Asia fell by 99.9 percent. The fall was caused by a drug given to cows. When cows were killed, the vultures fed on their remains (dead bodies). The drug in the cows' bodies was poisonous to the vultures.

Vultures helped clean up human garbage and **waste**. As the vultures died out, large packs of wild dogs took their place. These dogs carry the disease rabies, which can kill humans. The dogs have also attracted leopard predators. These leopards sometimes attack and kill children.

White-backed vultures were an important "clean-up squad" in many Asian cities.

Forest and Desert Food Webs

A forest food web

As we have seen (see page 26), we can look at **food chains** and **food webs** in different ways. One way shows how many total living things are at each level of a food chain or web. For a forest, this sort of "pyramid" is kite-shaped (see artwork below). Why is it small at the bottom like this? Trees are the **primary producer**. A few trees provide food (such as acorns) for many **consumers**.

But what if we were to look at this food web in terms of **biomass** or **energy** (see page 26)? The pyramid would be much larger at the bottom in both cases. Trees provide far more biomass (living material)—and energy —than the other levels of the pyramid.

This pyramid shows the number of living things in a forest food web.

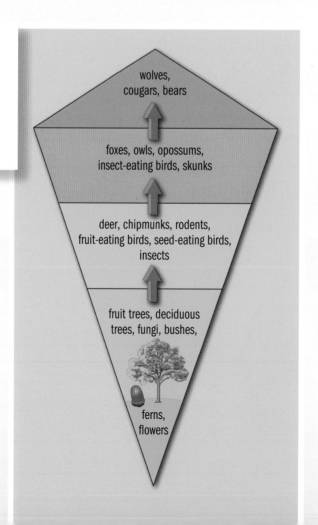

wolves, cougars, bears

foxes, owls, opossums, insect-eating birds, skunks

deer, chipmunks, rodents, fruit-eating birds, seed-eating birds, insects

fruit trees, deciduous trees, fungi, bushes,

ferns, flowers

A desert food web

The pyramid below is for a desert food web. Like the pyramid on page 42, it shows how many living things are at each level of the food chain or web in certain surroundings.

Desert food webs like this are very simple. Why? Because few **species** survive there. Deserts are very dry places. This means that plants find it hard to grow. Because plants are so rare, there is not much food for animals. So, there are not many animals in this food web. Most consumers are **ectothermic** (cold-blooded) animals such as insects. They need less energy—and food—to stay alive. Some large **mammals** find ways to survive, including camels. But there are fewer of them. That is why there is a small "point" of the pyramid below.

This pyramid shows the number of living things in a desert food web.

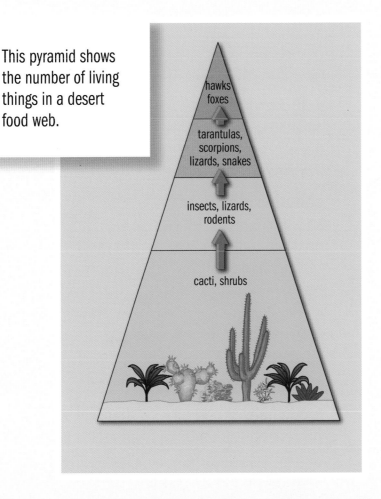

hawks
foxes

tarantulas,
scorpions,
lizards, snakes

insects, lizards,
rodents

cacti, shrubs

Glossary

algae group of plant-like living things that live mainly in water

bacterium (more than one: **bacteria**) type of single-celled living thing

biodiversity variety of life in the world or in a particular habitat

biomass dry weight of living material

biomass pyramid pyramid that shows the waste that happens between the steps of a food chain or web

camouflage colorings or markings that help an animal blend into the background

carbon dioxide substance in the air used by living things

cell building block of living things. It is the smallest unit of life.

cellulose substance that is important in plant cell walls

consumer living thing that eats other living things to get food

decomposer living thing that breaks down waste material and gets nutrients from it

detritus waste from other animals or plants

digest break food down into simpler substances that can be taken into the body

dung solid waste

ecological niche way of living and feeding within a habitat that allows a particular species to get food and survive

ectothermic describes an animal that gets heat from its surroundings to keep warm

endothermic describes an animal that produces heat within its body to keep its temperature constant, despite changes in the temperature of its surroundings

energy ability to do work

food chain group of living things that are connected through what they eat

food web group of living things that are connected through feeding relationships in a network

fungus (more than one: **fungi**) type of living thing that includes mushrooms and molds. Many fungi are decomposers.

glucose type of simple sugar

habitat surroundings in which a type of living thing lives

hydrogen sulfide poisonous gas with no color that smells of rotten eggs

hydrothermal vent hot spring deep on the seabed

keystone species species of plant or animal that is very important for a particular habitat

krill small, shrimp-like animal that lives in the sea

lignin tough, strong material produced in plants that is one of the main parts of wood

mammal warm-blooded animal with a backbone and fur or hair. Female mammals make milk to feed to their young.

migrate take a two-way journey, often between winter feeding and summer breeding sites (places where animals come together to have young)

nutrient useful part of food that living things use to live and grow

omnivore animal that eats both animals and plants

oxygen substance found in the air used by living things

photosynthesis process plants use to make food, using light energy from the Sun

phytoplankton very tiny living things found in the ocean, which are able to perform photosynthesis

pollen male plant reproductive cells

pollutant substance in an area that can cause illness or death in living things

predator animal that hunts other animals for food

prey animal that is hunted and eaten by animals for food

primary consumer plant-eater in a food chain or web

primary producer any living thing that can make its own food

quaternary consumer animal that eats tertiary consumers in a food chain or web

reproduce when a living thing makes copies of itself (has young)

respiration taking in oxygen and substances from food. These are combined in the cells. This process helps change food into energy.

rumen extra stomach in animals such as cows and sheep

secondary consumer animal that eats a primary consumer (plant-eater) in a food chain or web

snottite group of bacteria found in caves. These use substances like hydrogen sulfide in the cave—rather than sunlight—to make energy and food.

species group of similar living things that are able to have young with each other

tertiary consumer animal that eats secondary consumers (plant-eaters) in a food chain or web

urine liquid waste

vegetarian person or animal that eats only plant food

waste leftover, unwanted substance

zooplankton tiny sea animals

Find Out More

Books

Kalman, Bobbie. *What Are Food Chains and Webs?* (Science of Living Things). New York: Crabtree, 2009.

O'Donnell, Liam. *The World of Food Chains with Max Axiom, Super Scientist* (Graphic Library). North Mankato, Minn.: Capstone, 2007.

Rhodes, Mary Jo, and David Hall. *Life in a Kelp Forest* (Undersea Encounters). New York: Children's Press, 2005.

Solway, Andrew. *Food Chains and Webs: The Struggle to Survive* (Life Science). Vero Beach, Fla.: Rourke, 2008.

Spilsbury, Louise, and Richard Spilsbury. Food Webs series. Chicago: Heinemann Library, 2005.

Townsend, John. *Rotters!* (Life Processes and Living Things). Chicago: Raintree, 2006.

Websites

http://polardiscovery.whoi.edu/antarctica/ecosystem.html
Learn more about food webs in Antarctica.

http://video.nationalgeographic.com/video/player/kids/animals-pets-kids/ invertebrates-kids/krill-kids.html
Watch a video about krill and their place in food chains and webs.

www.geography4kids.com/files/land_foodchain.html
Learn more about food chains.

http://education.nationalgeographic.com/education/encyclopedia/ food-web/
National Geographic's website has lots of information about food chains and webs and related topics.

www.amnh.org
Explore the natural world on the American Museum of Natural History's website.

Topics to research

Temperature control

Find out more about endotherms and ectotherms. Mammals and birds are not the only animals that are endotherms. See if you can find out what other animals can keep themselves warm in cold conditions.

Phytoplankton

We know a lot about plants. But what about the living things that are the main producers in the oceans? Where are good places to find phytoplankton? Can you find the names of three different kinds? A good place to start is in the Arctic or Antarctic. See, for example, http://nsidc. org/seaice/environment/phytoplankton.html.

Parasites

Parasites are an interesting part of the food web. Can you find out about common human parasites? What about parasites on other animals?

Index